Practical Primary Drama

Practical Primary Drama

Geoff Davies

HEINEMANN EDUCATIONAL BOOKS

Heinemann Educational Books Ltd
22 Bedford Square, London WC1B 3HH
LONDON EDINBURGH MELBOURNE AUCKLAND
HONG KONG SINGAPORE KUALA LUMPUR NEW DELHI
IBADAN NAIROBI JOHANNESBURG
PORTSMOUTH (NH) KINGSTON PORT OF SPAIN

First published 1983
Reprinted 1985

Cover design by Alan Chalk

British Library Cataloguing in Publication Data

Davies, G.C.
    Practical primary drama.
    1. Drama in education
    I. Title
    372.6'6   PN3171

    ISBN 0-435-18236-6

Set by The Castlefield Press of Northampton
Printed and bound in Great Britain by
Biddles Ltd, Guildford and King's Lynn

Contents

Acknowledgements

I would like to thank the headteachers, staff, and children of Whinney Banks Infant School, Middlesbrough, Green Gates Primary School, Redcar and West Dyke Primary School, Redcar; also Mrs Ann Nakash, Mrs Denise Stanton, Mrs Joan Hendry for helpful suggestions; Mrs Sheila Anderson and Miss Patricia Grey of Middlesbrough Teachers Centre who prepared the first draft, and my wife who read everything.

Most of all, my grateful thanks to all those Cleveland teachers with whom I have worked or who have attended the many courses and conferences with which I have been associated and to whom this book is dedicated.

1 Introduction

Why there is a need for this book

Over the last four or five years, a number of books have been published on Drama in Education which have completely redefined the subject and placed it squarely in the centre of the curriculum rather than as an extra curricula option. In place of the *teaching* of drama, the emphasis is now on *learning* through drama. However, although this new theory of drama in education has been intensively analysed, very little has been written about the problems associated with putting these theories into practice. In my job as Head of a Teachers Centre, being involved in various drama in education courses, I am regularly being asked to recommend a really down to earth book which gives sound practical advice. I have to admit that to my knowledge such a book does not, as yet, exist. The demand for help in doing drama with younger children, I have found, is very great. Teachers in primary schools are well aware of the value of drama as an activity but many are unsure of how to go about it. Many try but give up owing to a lack of early success. As a result, despite the claims made for the activity as an educational aid, drama is not as widespread as one might suppose. Books about the teaching of drama often contain examples of ways of starting drama using games and exercises. These are explained as preparing the children for drama, creating the right atmosphere and attitudes. When the children are ready then drama can start. These books rarely tell you what to do when the drama actually starts. Underlining this approach is the assumption that drama is a particularly difficult activity which requires special conditions and qualities. As a result, many teachers spend precious time each week doing these games and exercises rather than doing drama itself. Many children never get to the point where they are ever actually engaged in drama at all.

In this book, drama is seen as a valuable educational tool. It can be used to develop insights within a particular area of the curriculum, for example, history or geography. It can be employed in the classroom to encourage creative writing and art and to help children to develop language. It can give them confidence and practice in solving problems, making decisions and working co-operatively. Through drama, a special kind of learning can take place. By becoming involved actively in make-believe, children are engaged in direct experience. Certain things happen during drama which do not happen when doing anything else, so the earlier children start the better.

To be able to read or to write, children have to learn a series of special skills but to do drama there are no obstacles to overcome, no complex concepts or skills required. Every child already possesses, almost from birth, all the necessary requirements. In fact, most children spontaneously do drama in their everyday playing long before they come to school. Again, unlike many other subjects, drama does not require any special facilities or conditions, books or equipment—it is the cheapest activity on the curriculum. It is not necessary either to use the school hall as good drama can take place just as easily in the classroom. All you need is a teacher, some children and a space.

However, because every class will be different, it is not possible, in a book, to provide model lessons guaranteed to work. In fact, the very essence of learning through drama is that it is the particular group of children who create the action. Drama is a corporate, creative activity, so the drama is a reflection, first, of the children and second of the teacher, his or her values, experience, training, status and self-image. Each individual lesson is also subject to the particular context—the time of the year and day, the previous activity, the condition of the room. All these are influenced by the school's environment and ethos, the age and composition of the class, their general ability and social health and the relationship between teacher and pupils. So each lesson will be different even if the topic is the same. This book is not about preparing for drama but actually doing it, i.e.—children and teacher in an imaginary situation that they all accept, taking on roles and living through an experience.

How I came to use drama in my teaching

I had been teaching for six years before I ever considered drama as a classroom activity. Drama, for me, was simply the putting on of plays at Christmas and I'd done a little of that without becoming particularly enthusiastic. In a primary school in Rochdale I had been allocated to the remedial class, a collection of those children who could not cope with the work in the other classes. They were of mixed ages, from 7–11 with various learning difficulties, which boiled down for the headteacher to the fact that they could not read. There were only 28 children in the class, which in those days, I considered quite small but despite having a part-time teacher helping in the morning, my predecessor had given up after having a nervous breakdown.

On the staff of this school was a teacher recently out of college, who had studied 'Drama-Mains' and the drama adviser for Rochdale was making a special effort to keep in touch with teachers who were likely to do drama in their schools. He, therefore, spent quite a lot of time at the school taking lessons or observing. I didn't like the idea of members of remedial classes being separated from their peers all the time and so I arranged for some of the children to return to their age-group class with me for certain activities, one of which was drama. I can't fully describe my amazement at what I saw. Drama seemed to be an activity which everybody could do well. Although it was a highly structured type of drama teaching, all the children enjoyed themselves, making up plays, taking on roles and acting out situations. The important point was that my small group from the remedial class could do this as well as anyone. Although they were continually seen as failures in reading, in drama they could experience success. After this I became more and more involved in these drama lessons, started to attend a Saturday morning drama club in the town and gradually began to do drama on my own with my own class.

I left that school after only one year because I was promoted to what today would be called a Scale 3 post in Teesside. When I first walked into the staffroom, I sensed that teachers were all giving me rather funny looks. I soon discovered why. This large junior school was still a three-stream school and I was given 4C and everybody knew it. 'A bunch of future inmates of Durham Prison' was how one teacher described them. I soon discovered, however, that basically school had failed them and so I tried to give to them what was called compensatory education. Included in this was a hefty slice of drama of all types including regular class productions, some of which were performed for the parents. One of these was a Passion Play with the biggest villain in the school playing Jesus Christ. 'I'd like to . . . crucify him', was one teacher's comment on hearing the casting. The Last Supper scene followed the interval. Everything was carefully laid out on the table, including blackcurrant juice and crusty bread. Unfortunately, there was some delay so that when Act 2 eventually started, the bread and wine had disappeared down the throats of the twelve apostles.

It was while I was at this school, that I went on my first drama course, run by Teesside College of Education and although the actual course work was useful, I learned even more from listening to the other course members and what they were doing in drama in their schools.

In September 1971, I became deputy head of a junior school (7–11) and suggested that all the classes in the school should do at least some drama. The headteacher agreed with this although his expectations of school drama at that time were more akin to amateur dramatics. Of course, I was also involved in all the other aspects of the curriculum as every primary teacher has to be, so that drama was still only a small part of my work.

One thing which always impressed me was that after a drama session, unlike after a maths lesson, I was rarely tired. In fact, I always felt elated, wanting to talk about what had just happened. Usually when teachers talk during break times, it is either nothing to do with education or is bemoaning the deficiencies of the children in their class. To have somebody who wants to describe every detail of lessons is a bit too much for some teachers.

In 1973 I was granted secondment to attend the one-year diploma course in Drama in Education run by Dorothy Heathcote at the University of Newcastle.

Later, the school I was teaching in changed from a junior (7–11) to a primary school (5–11) and we were all introduced to a strange new animal—the infant. At first we had only one group of 30 reception children and so there appeared an immense gap between these 'babies' and the first-year juniors. They seemed so tiny that the rest of the children in the school treated the newcomers like dolls, cuddling them, giving them swings and donkey rides and generally providing maternal protection.

A group of juniors would 'adopt' an infant and in the playground could be seen catering for their every need—tying shoelaces or ribbons and escorting them to the toilet.

Gradually, however, it dawned on us that these newcomers were not the 'little angels' that we at first imagined. When one 'sweet' child discovered that if you kicked a junior nobody kicked you back, he went on a rampage kicking as many as possible—('Isn't this fun, Mother?'). Others became petty tyrants demanding instant obedience of their junior slaves. The novelty began to wear off and we all began to agree, that, as one junior boy said to me, 'Some of them are little devils', i.e. they are just people but smaller—with the 'good, the bad and the ugly'.

It was one of my jobs to try to integrate the growing numbers of infants into the school, and as I used to do drama with the juniors, I thought I would therefore try some with the infants.

Thinking, in my innocence, that they had been brought up on a diet of 'Listen with Mother' and such, I initially worked on traditional themes taken from nursery rhymes and fairy stories. I was therefore most put out when, with the interest low and response poor, the drama lessons were not very successful. Take-off occurred by accident when a session concerned with 'going on our holidays by plane' changed dramatically when we were hi-jacked. I was amazed at how much they knew of such things as dynamite, bazookas, guns, hostages, helicopters and parachutes—'sweet, innocent children'?

As the numbers of infants increased in the school so did my experience and knowledge of the most appropriate drama for them. I could never be certain what topics would be attractive beforehand, and so the most effective lessons were those where the topic was chosen by the children themselves and I followed their initiatives and used their ideas.

Children, of course, vary enormously in their interests and in what they are capable of. It is true that many are attracted by nursery rhymes and fairy stories but there are just as many who are interested in Batman, James Bond and Starsky and Hutch—and who is to say which is more wholesome? Just consider Little Red Riding Hood or Three Little Pigs for example.

The first problem was the constraints of an established story line. Dramatizing a known story was obviously popular, but very soon I found myself talking in theatrical terms about how well or badly they acted their part.

For me, the real drama started when on one occasion we had to go through Little Red Riding Hood's forest—into the unknown. From here a new story began, with no prescribed ending, created by the children in response to the new situation.

What is drama in education?

One of the main aims of drama in education is to develop the children's imaginative thinking. It is the children who should be challenged to produce the ideas, of which they are quite capable if the teacher provides the necessary stimulus. This stimulus need not be anything elaborate but could be simply the right questions.

Before this is possible, the teacher has to discover the level of thinking in the class and to provide an atmosphere where what each individual has to say is regarded as important in itself.

Questions must be sufficiently open to challenge the children's thinking, stimulating a response without suggesting that there is only one answer. Also there is a need to avoid the implication that only certain subjects are legitimate in drama (i.e. teacher's subjects). It must become clear that their interests are always important enough to be considered. As I discovered, it is so easy to underestimate children, to proceed on the basis that their experience is so short and narrow as to offer little or nothing. Even the youngest children have something to offer if they feel confident enough that their ideas will be considered. Every child has experience to draw on even if this at first appears to be derived solely from television. Whole areas of knowledge and experience remain untapped unless the teacher can provide the opportunity and the occasion for these to be utilized.

I am regularly impressed by the depth of knowledge and understanding displayed by young children who, I have been informed, are not capable of very much.

Here is an example from a first-year infant class:

This class had decided to do a journey into space.

> 'Where shall we go?' asks the teacher.
> 'Let's go to the sun,' says a little boy.
> 'We can't do that,' replies another.
> 'Why?' asks the teacher.
> 'Because it's too hot,' replies a girl.
> 'We'd get burned up,' says another.
> 'It seems we can't go to the sun,' says the teacher to the little boy who had made the original suggestion.
> 'Yes we can,' he answers.
> 'How?' asks the teacher.
> 'We make a rocket out of special stuff that protects us from the heat,' he replies.
> 'Do you think we can make our rocket like that?' the teacher asks the class.
> 'Oh yes,' many say.
> 'What shall we make it out of?'
> 'Asbestos,' says one little boy (a six-year-old).

The properties of asbestos would not normally be regarded as appropriate to the curriculum of a second-year primary class but a piece of knowledge never before considered of value, suddenly became relevant in response to the need created by the drama situation. And it is because these situations become so real to the children that any problems which do arise need to be solved for their own sake or so that the 'pretend' world will continue. They do not have to be solved to please teacher or to get good marks but because it is important to the children themselves.

This class of reception children wanted to catch a dragon.

> 'How are we going to do that?'
> 'We'll dig a big hole for the dragon to fall down.'
> The class proceed to dig the large imaginary hole in the middle of the hall.
> 'But the dragon will see the hole.'
> 'We'll have to cover the hole with twigs and grass to make it invisible.'
> 'How do we know the dragon will come this way?' asks the teacher.
> 'We must put some bait near the hole.'
> 'What can we use as bait?'
> 'Have you got anything?'
> 'I've got some sweets.'
> 'Will sweets do?' asks the teacher.
> 'Oh yes,' everyone agrees.
> The class and teacher go and hide.
> 'If you hear anything, let us know.'
> After a short wait:
> 'I think we've caught something.'
> The class rush out to look into the hole.
> 'What have we caught?' asks the teacher.
> 'It's only a baby dragon.'
> Everyone is disappointed.
> 'Why do you think we've only caught a baby dragon?'
> 'I know,' says a little girl.
> 'Why?' asks the teacher.
> 'Well, children like sweets more than adults so probably

baby dragons like sweets more than grown-up dragons.'
'So what do you think grown-up dragons like?' etc, etc. . . .

What was involved here was not only the attempt to solve the initial problem but also the opportunity to see the consequences of that decision and the attempt to rectify the error and try again.

None of this can be achieved unless all the class plus teacher are engaged in one dramatic situation and subject to the same constraints. I often find that junior teachers are reluctant to 'make a fool of themselves' and get involved, but most infant teachers include 'pretending' as a regular part of the school day and therefore have little trouble becoming part of an imaginary situation. Drama, unfortunately, is still too strongly associated with acting and the theatre, and that involvement by the teacher means having *to act*, a skill, which, quite naturally, many teachers do not possess. In fact, this is the one talent that is *not* required. To take on a role does not involve strange ways of talking or funny walks but the ability to look at a situation from another's viewpoint—i.e. to stand in someone else's shoes, but not necessarily to be another person.

And the role that the teacher assumes is crucial. Without the teacher, the children will not be able to achieve the depth of thinking and imaginative involvement that is possible in primary drama and which is so vital if drama is to be of value in the education of the primary school child.

Drama is not an easy option. It could be the most difficult activity the children are asked to do at school. It demands full and complete concentration on their part. They will be faced with real life problems for which there are no easy answers.
For example: 'How do you make a person happy?'
                'How do you know how to trust a person?'
                'How do you choose a leader?'
They have to think deeply not only as individuals but also as members of a group. And teacher is not there as the person 'who knows all' but is sharing the experience, asking the difficult questions, challenging assumptions, not directing or giving orders.

2 The Drama Session _or_ How I Do Drama

Meeting the class

My drama teaching is now carried out in various different schools so when I am to do drama for the first time with a class, I need to consider three questions: What do they know of me? What do they expect? What does _drama_ mean to them?

I always start by asking a class if they know who I am and what I do (I naturally get some funny answers at times). If they say that I do drama, I ask them whether they have done drama before. 'What is drama?' I ask. The word drama obviously means many different things, ranging from fighting and killing to movement, miming, acting or doing plays. If I don't get many replies to this question I sometimes rephrase it by saying 'Drama on ITV' or 'Drama in the North Sea'—'What do you think that might be about?'

My main aim is to get a positive response from the class. I very rarely find a class who have never heard or seen the word somewhere or sometime. Whatever response I do get, I say something like, 'Do you think we could do drama here today?' or 'Would you like to do some drama?' Sometimes I give the class my definition of drama, which is people pretending to be someone else, or somewhere else, or both.

'Are you good at pretending? Do you think we could pretend we are somewhere else? Instead of being in your school hall, could we pretend we are somewhere very different? Is that easy or hard? Can we forget that the piano is over there and the dinner tables are piled up in the corner? You can! What sort of place shall we pretend to be in?' And the ideas come.

If I start by asking 'Can you pretend to be someone else?', the response will be to split up the class which at this stage I want to avoid. My aim is to gain some general agreement as to what we are doing. That is, we are going to have an adventure together. I suspect that not all are in favour or some are not too sure, it is important to either reassure them or to make some temporary contact with them. I might say 'Shall we give it a try and then after half an hour we will have a talk about it and you can tell me whether you liked it or not or even, if you like, you watch and join in when you feel ready.' Sometimes, I might have a few short trial runs, such as for a few minutes pretending we are in a jungle or on the beach or carrying a heavy weight or suffering from a bad leg or anything they suggest. Then we stop, gather round and discuss what we have just been doing. 'Did you enjoy that? Did you find it easy or hard? Did you find it silly?' I cannot see any purpose in going on unless I have this agreement that we are to try drama. It depends on the children. You can't do it alone or by giving orders. The children are going to be involved in creating a story together—a corporate, creative process. It is worth spending time gaining their confidence and support because without it drama is a waste of time.

Starting the drama
When you feel that the class are prepared to go along with the idea of trying drama, you then have to find ways of edging them gradually into a full pretend situation. After, because of their natural ability to pretend and their constant enjoyment of imaginative play, young children fall into a full acceptance of the make-believe with little effort on your part. If this is the case then all you have to do is provide a stimulus or a starting point. Sometimes all you need to ask the class is 'Where shall we start?' or 'What shall we make a play about?' If they look ready and eager to start, rather than discuss, I ask them whether they would mind if I pretend to be someone else. If they agree and accept the idea (and you can easily tell if they are unready for this by embarrassed giggling and looks), I say that I am going to go over there and think for a minute and then return as this other

person. I say, 'You will soon guess who I am from what I say. I'm not going to dress up or put on a funny voice or walk.' Then I say, 'You will also find out who or what you are as I go along. Are you ready?' When I think they are ready I duly go over, wait quietly with my back to them (all the time listening for clues as to their readiness—Are they quiet? Are they giggling or talking?). When I return I do not introduce myself. I talk as if they already know who I am and what they are. Usually I am a person who has a problem, difficulty or weakness and the class have been specially chosen because of their particular qualities or expertise. I try to avoid making the problem, the situation, the mime, or their roles too specific at this stage. The children must be allowed to build up the drama at their own pace according to their interests, knowledge, understanding, or social cohesion. You must listen to their responses and reactions. Can they cope with this? Are they with you?

The immediate response might be that they find teacher too much to take. They again might giggle or look puzzled or remain completely dumb in awe. If this happens then there is no point in going on. You must stop and find out why. Usually this is because they haven't understood what you said earlier and not really knowing what to expect were taken by surprise. It is, therefore, very important to take on a very low-key role (no histrionics), as near as possible to yourself but sufficient for them to see the difference. Moreover, it must be a sympathetic character to whom they can relate, asking for help, making the class feel important, specially chosen.

If they accept you in this role then your function from then on is to allow the children to assume roles gradually at their pace— no casting.

Role taking does not mean becoming a character as in a film or a play but assuming the mantle of some expertise or knowledge.

'Does anyone here know anything about pigs? Do you know how to run a circus? Can anybody here milk a cow? Was anyone here sent from the space station?' Many questions like this will get no response so you have to keep trying until you do. This process is about finding out what they know and understand.

The drama can only proceed on their suggestions even though they might not be accurate. They have to build up the setting and you have to utilize this. I once had a farm which had potatoes in one field and bananas in the next. It is important at this stage not to be the one who knows (the teacher role) because if you do the ideas will dry up. You are a person who has a problem and they have the answers, if they exist. Don't make it too easy. It comes from them. Accept everything you receive and put it to the rest of the class for their opinions. 'Do you think that will work? Shall we do that then?'

Other ways of starting
Role-playing is very difficult for some teachers. Maybe they only feel safe playing the teacher role and therefore departing from this security is too big a risk. Having seen many teachers trying, there are other obvious dangers. Some over-act and become ridiculous—the class stops and laughs. Some are so good the class feel inhibited, feel they cannot compete with teacher and so do nothing. Others only take on a role which is so similar to the teacher's that they lose any advantage that could be gained from role play. Role play offers certain possibilities that the teacher role is denied, one of which is not being the fount of all knowledge.

It might be preferable, therefore, for the idea of playing a different role to creep up on the children almost without them knowing, so another way of starting must be used. Often children are used to doing movement or mime so this could be used as a starting point.

'Find a space and then let's walk around the room. Let's change it to that you have hurt your leg. Stop. You are carrying a heavy weight on your back. What could you be carrying? Where would we be? In a jungle, desert, mountain? Will you lead? Are there any dangers on this journey? Do you think we should check that we have all the things we need?'

Each one of these questions narrows down the area of concern and leads towards a focus which we have not found yet. Each question also provides a need for some discussion leading to a decision which provides the reason for action.

(Notice that in this method there is no mention of role, I use 'we' to reinforce the fact that 'we' are 'us' but in a different place.)

The children as a group are slowly building up the place according to what they know and understand and what they can cope with. It might be a jungle or a mountain about which they know very little from direct experience but perhaps a great deal from books, pictures and television, knowledge which is often very superficial. You have to attempt to make it as real as possible so that all can believe. The problem will be that each child will have a different image, a different picture in their mind, different levels of interest and commitment.

How can you provide some focus which will give the whole class a common experience, a shared image? If this is thought necessary then you have a number of options depending on a range of factors. I usually latch on to one idea from a child and make sure the whole class is aware. I might say 'He said that there are wild animals in this wood' or 'Won't the pirates see our footprints?' or 'How can we prevent the dragon from escaping?' These are problems that all must solve and therefore, must think about.

Sometimes everybody doing the same thing helps to build up this group-togetherness, i.e. digging trenches, building walls or putting up tents.

Sometimes after a period attempting to encourage the children to use their imaginations (liberate their creativity) too many ideas may be produced, with too much happening. You, therefore, have to narrow the focus and firm up certain ideas as opposed to others, which may be shelved. It may be necessary to concentrate on something practical which all can understand— lighting fires, cooking a meal and eating it, cleaning your gun. If there is any reticence on the part of some of the children, others may be used to demonstrate in the context of the story. 'Is there anyone who can show us how to put up our tent so that it is not blown down by the wind?'

Sometimes it may be necessary to involve the whole class in certain activities where everyone does exactly the same. It may be the crossing of a swamp when there is only one route. Either I or one of the children show the way and all follow on a dangerous journey drama, the whole group make their way along a narrow ledge holding hands. Each of these methods serves the purpose of uniting the group while also allowing each child to discover the game that is being played. They must come to accept the basic rules of the medium of drama by seeing the reason for doing it. Fundamentally they must feel comfortable and safe and be enjoying themselves. It must not appear silly. If they see that the teacher takes the whole thing seriously then the children will also.

Once you have them accepting both you and the activity you then have to see what they are capable of. Can they work as a whole group without you? Can they quickly form small groups and work well in these groups? Are some children left out of groups, isolated? Do they like working as individuals? Do the boys work with the girls? How much help do they need from you? When there is a discussion, does every idea come through you? Do they listen to each other?

The only way to find out the answers to these questions is to give the children the opportunity to show you.

Ask them to form up into groups of say four or five spread out in the hall and discuss the problem at issue and then watch them very carefully. How long does it take for them to get into groups? Is it a very noisy affair? Do they fall naturally into friendship groups? Are all groups mixed and when they are together do they begin to talk or do they withhold answers or have their arms around each other's shoulders, do they fall about on the floor or slide around, or do they sit looking lost at each other?

You might, therefore, have to do this very slowly, not quite like counting in fours, but almost. Get one group and show them how you would like them to form themselves and sit. Say very clearly what they have to discuss and how each person must be given the opportunity to voice their opinion. Tell them that they have to come to a decision and that one of the group will be asked to tell all the other groups what this decision is.

This process might take a long time (I hope it's not necessary) but it is well worth the effort for later occasions.

Good all-group discussions are of great value in drama but if everybody talks at once and nobody listens, they are a waste of time. The teacher must make it clear that the aim of the discussion is to find out what they think, that everyone's opinion is important. First of all, ask a simple question, though not an easy one. 'What shall we wear?' As you receive replies make a note of them (on a blackboard or paper or your fingers). Go through the replies so that everyone hears. Get the class to examine each one so that equal attention is devoted to each suggestion. When an opinion is expressed either echo it or preferably say, 'What do you think of that idea?' If they do not respond say, 'Bryan, could you repeat that idea so that everyone can hear?' 'Now what do you think, do you like that idea?' The aim is to make listening important. You can say, 'I thought I heard a great idea down here but other people were talking so I couldn't tell what it was. If we all speak one at a time then we will hear all the ideas and nothing will be lost.' Use the tension of the drama. 'The idea that we didn't hear might be the one that saves our lives' or 'This is important, the pirates will be here soon.'

The vital thing is to make it very clear that their ideas are the important ones and not yours. You must accept all their ideas however silly they might sound at first. Your job is to organize, clarify and amplify their ideas, not to pass judgement. You must, therefore, ask a new type of question—a non-teacher question where you genuinely want their opinions because you cannot know the answers.

A new type of question
Often teachers ask questions of children solely to test their knowledge—the teacher knows the answer. Children answer for various reasons, including wanting to please teacher, or do not answer because they might get it wrong.

Questions in drama must be genuine questions requiring facts or opinions from the children. 'What shall we do drama about?' 'What shall we pretend today?'

The children will begin to see the difference only when you demonstrate that the answers they give are treated with *due reverence*. They will soon latch on to you if you have already made your mind up. All the answers must be collected and given equal attention. Write them on a blackboard, count them out on your fingers, ask individual children to remember particular ideas. I once asked a class what we should do our play about and wrote out a list which became almost a syllabus for the half term. The list was Frankenstein, Dracula, Werewolves, Ghosts, and King Kong. Each week we did a different one and ticked the title off the list which was written on the blackboard.

Useful questions at this stage are those which offer alternatives or narrow down the options.
Examples: 'Would you want a play about helping people in trouble or being the people in trouble?'
'Do you want to be scared or to scare others?'
'Do you want to be in the castle or outside trying to get in?'

If you get too many ideas, the best plan is to put the problem to the children, 'What shall we choose for today or this week and which shall we leave aside for now—we can't do them all?' Ideas must never be rejected by the teacher although he or she can have an opinion. I'm afraid that I am often guilty of saying 'We did that last week or last term'. If you are faced with a number of suggestions with equal support you can sometimes combine ideas. Three ideas—a robbery, a supermarket, and a ship became a robbery of the duty free shop on an ocean liner.

How do you decide?
The best way is to sense the degree of interest. Do their faces light up? Do they nod their heads and start talking agitatedly with their neighbour or do they look rather deadpan? Supplementary questions will reveal what they are really thinking when they make a suggestion. When they say 'Ghosts' or 'The Seaside' or whatever, is it something on television, a project at school, something they've done before, or simply a word? Do they really know something about it? If they say 'Pirates' do they want to be pirates or do they want to meet pirates? What sort of pirates? Doing what? By asking more

questions the degree of interest can be gauged more accurately. Sometimes I say 'Let's have a try' and we get up and spread out round the room. If the choice was between 'Witches', 'Being on an Island' or 'In the Baths', we try this out. We find a space and all become witches. Witches walking, stirring, making spells, being nasty, etc.

Then perhaps, landing on an island to explore—'What did you find?' 'What is it like on this island?' 'Does anyone live here, what sort of people are they, where do they live?' etc. And then a similar range of activities connected with going to the baths.

Then you bring the class together and ask again what they enjoyed doing the most and what they think might offer the most potential for the drama.

Sometimes the group can get so involved in one of these activities that they forget that they are only in a 'trying it out' period and continue with this until the end of the session.

Another approach using action might be:
1. Walk around this room as yourself.
2. Imagine you had an accident on the way to school and you hurt some part of your body which still hurts—carry on walking.
3. Imagine you are carrying something very heavy in your pack—what do you think this could be—we are still walking.
4. Try and imagine that we are walking where the ground is not as small and hard as the hall floor. What sort of place could this be? e.g. rough hills, forest.
5. 'Why might we be in a place like this and what are we carrying? Have we got all we need? Shall we go on? Who will lead the way?' or 'Would you like to collect your equipment and I'll come and look at it?' . . . and the drama is off the ground.

The decision—'and now the crunch'
If this does not happen and you are no nearer to a decision then a vote might have to be taken or an arrangement made whereby all suggestions will be done in order—a commitment you must keep

to maintain credibility. If you do have to have a vote, it must be made clear that the class will agree to do the drama decided by the largest number—no opting out if the vote is lost. It is amazing how often the voting itself becomes the drama mainly because this is such a new experience.

Many teachers understand the concept of the children deciding as being 'letting the children do what they want'. What is really meant is giving the children responsibility for their own learning. Responsibility is the key word. In effect this means allowing the children to decide on the content of the lesson. What it does not mean is the abnegation of responsibility for the structure and organization of the lesson. This must be maintained throughout. In a sense, the children could do 'pirates' every week but each time it will be different. This difference will be caused by the questioning and structure by the teacher. The children must be made to see the implications behind their suggestions and answers so that they will give them sufficient thought. They must give greater consideration to the others in the class because what they do governs what happens next and if it is no good then they bear the responsibility. In other words, far more is being asked of them than simply doing what the teacher says.

3 What Happens in Drama?

The functions of the teacher

Drama in many primary schools means simply the Nativity Play once a year or a five-minute dramatic presentation for assembly. Sometimes it is the music and movement type lesson with the teacher giving a series of instructions to which the children respond, often like puppets. To attempt anything else terrifies some teachers. Most teachers approach the subject with great caution. It may present problems of control, of structuring the work and of developing new kinds of relationships with children. A drama lesson can never be planned down to the last detail. It is not always easy to assess what has been achieved. Working with children's own experience and knowledge and entering their fantasy world involves too great a risk. I believe that this risk is worth taking. Gradually the benefits will become too obvious to ignore.

What then is the function of the teacher in drama lessons? First, helping the children to choose a topic which is acceptable to the majority of the class. Often this will have been suggested by some incident in the classroom, by a story or a television programme. Once started it is possible for a class to continue with one 'story' or drama theme for a whole term so that each session is a continuation of the one before. Each drama session does not need to have (like a good story) a beginning, middle, and end. Each situation needs to be considered as it comes and not as part of some all-enhancing whole.

The story as such is not important so a teacher need not worry about making progress. What matters is the level of thinking and the degree of involvement. Only if the situation does not appear to be interesting or challenging enough should the teacher attempt to move on. The 'trapping a dragon' drama related earlier went on for six sessions over as many weeks and we still did not catch ourselves a dragon.

What is required for each lesson is a focus—usually a problem. Often the previous lesson provided the need for some research (yes, research with infants). You may have needed to discover for example 'What do you feed crocodiles?' or 'How do you get a parrot to talk?' or 'What makes a witch happy?' The answer or possible answer to such questions forms the new starting point and creates a new situation.

It is very easy, however, to fall into the trap of directing and giving orders. It will, of course, always look more orderly and appear, at least superficially, more satisfying. Everybody will look busy and involved. If it stays like this though, it will become educationally a rather useless activity. The children will either sit and wait for the next instruction or start to be naughty.

It is very important to resist the temptation to provide the answers and the ideas. You must structure the activity and frame the questions but in a different way from normal.

If the children are being asked to pretend or imagine they are somewhere else or are somebody else, then you must do the same and this must be made clear to the class. I always ask the children if they would mind my being a particular person, e.g. the farmer or circus owner or I tell them I am going to be someone else, then try it out, stop and ask them what they felt.

At first, this new person probably appears very much like teacher. It is a great mistake to act or 'ham it up' with a funny voice and silly walk. Anything like this will either make the children laugh or turn them into an audience for teacher's 'amateur dramatics'. The essence of the activity is 'role play'— the assumption of the position of someone with duties, responsibilities, rights and problems, e.g. captain of the ship, owner of the farm, king or queen. What is not required is the stereotype or caricature—the Hollywood image. Every king has to rule but every king is different.

The children then must not be put off by teacher in role. On the contrary, the teacher in role must reassure the children in their make-believe world; make it legitimate. By seeing the teacher in role, they come to a better understanding of what being in role would mean for them. You might say:

'My home is in a terrible mess, could you help me clear it for the visit of the Queen?'   *or*

'Will you help me get my circus going again?'   *or*

'If you want some of the treasure, you must help me search for it.'

Your main responsibility is to find a role within the drama that allows you to control the situation without having to provide all the ideas. Sometimes this may mean being the leader but it is more productive if the children are in some way cast as the experts while you are in need of their expertise. A class, with whom I was working, took on the role of agricultural experts; I was a farmer. I was once a man who had been left a circus in a will and did not know how to run it. I have been a man from the Council who had the job of designing a children's playground. Taking on roles such as these, the problem can be presented to the children, discussed and acted upon. The task which follows will create new problems and a different focus. The initial problem concerned the whole class but the task itself may demand that the children work in groups. As a result, new problems will arise which may concern only one group or even one child. In the example of the farm, mentioned earlier, the group in charge of poultry found that the chickens were not laying. As they did not know the solution to this problem, the whole class was consulted (How do you get chickens to lay?). The children then have the opportunity to operate as individuals, in pairs or in groups while contributing to an overall situation in which the teacher is involved and is able, when necessary, to apply the pressure and deepen the experience.

Unless this function is performed by you, the drama will tend to be superficial and may skip about from topic to topic without delving into the implications of any of them. With the teacher in the drama, each situation can be fully explored and no problem overcome until a carefully considered decision has been made which is then seen to be executed.

When and where to start

The best opportunity to start is during that almost universal part of the school day in every primary school—storytime. Most teachers try to avoid having a passive audience by attempting to involve children with such questions as

'What do you think happened next?'   *or*

'What would you do?'

Often children have favourite stories and demand that they be read over and over again so that they know exactly what is to come (even the exact word). These stories are often dramatized in classes with each child getting a chance to play the lead. There is no doubt that children enjoy doing this but I do not think that this is making the best use of the story.

For a change, ask the class if they would like to meet someone from the story. If, for example, the story is *Cinderella*, tell the class that you are going to be one of the ugly sisters or Buttons. You might begin by saying—'Have you heard what's happened to my sister Cinderella?' Or as Buttons, 'Cinderella used to be my friend and now she has gone to live in the palace.'

Drama like this may only last five minutes but it is likely to have started the children talking and thinking in fresh ways.

Dressing up—usefulness and limitations

To play and pretend comes easily to most children and dressing up can be an important part. Many classrooms have a well-used dressing-up box. Left to themselves, the children will use the items in a tremendous variety of ways. The key to success lies in having items of clothing which are not too specific in their use or application. Squares of material of different colours and textures rather than mother's party dresses or hats. Keep a special lookout for things like cloaks or anything made of interesting or luxurious fabrics. Using these items, children will play privately without any need for any intervention from teacher.

In drama sessions, however, dressing-up clothes and props

can be a great hindrance to the development of the imagination. The danger is that children can come to believe that this cannot be another person without the correct clothes or the right accessories. Everything thus has to be real or acceptably real. The pirate has to have his cutlass, every soldier a gun, the spaceman his suit. If the room is a house, then it must have a kitchen and bedroom. Very soon, most of the drama time is taken up with the dressing-up of each character and preparing the space. Chairs and tables begin to appear together with props of every shape and size to clutter the area. Most of these objects do not mean very much to most of the class and simply get in the way. All this distracts from the important thing which is what is going on in the children's heads.

The basic theory to be remembered, is that whatever and whenever they pretend is real in their minds. The house is a real house, the ship is real, if they say so. We will believe if it is important to believe.

This of course demands great concentration and effort. The room can be anything at anytime. It can change regularly and instantly. The snow-covered mountain becomes a base camp; the forest becomes a castle. An intruder passing through the hall will not see anything—only those involved. It is a secret imaginary world. Doing drama this way means that you can not only change the setting but also change roles. Drama is very valuable in providing opportunities for children to see both sides of a situation. Being Red Indians attacking a wagon train one minute or one session, and then being the settlers. Who is right? Whose land is this anyway? Drama is basically about people playing particular roles in life and finding out what it is like.

Props and costumes, however, do have a place. I believe they should come after an exploratory session where perhaps it was decided to examine in detail the lives of a particular group of people. For a drama on Red Indians, one class made headbands from strips of light card and designed a symbol for their tribal names, such as, Sharp Eyes, Bald Eagle, Running Water. These simple props symbolized for the children their identity within the story. In a drama about a market place, each group had a stall sign and their name.

One large group or several small groups?
It is not always possible or advisable for all the class to work all
the time as one big group. Sometimes inspired by a common
stimulus, children will want to work in smaller groups or as
individuals. You will not always be aware of everything that is
going on. For example, the class decide to help the incompetent
circus owner. One group looks after the lions, another the
elephants, while others practice on the trapeze. In a class of 35,
there may be over a dozen different activities demanding space.
In real life this would require a large field. With only a small hall
or classroom, each child or group create their own space for their
own imaginary drama. Everything is possible in the mind. The
rule is—don't clutter up the area, allow the imagination to flow.

Your task, therefore, involves a continual process of class
organization and re-organization. Full discussions especially
with a class of 40 can present many difficulties. Children need to
be trained not only to think and express their own ideas but also
to listen and respond to other peoples'. A system must be
arranged so that only one child speaks at a time and all who want
to, have a chance to speak. To avoid duplication it is a good idea
to write down all suggestions on a blackboard or large sheet of
paper so that nothing is forgotten or ignored. If there is a strong
difference of opinion and a decision has to be made, then a
formal vote may be required. Rarely will all this be possible first
time round but children can be trained to abide by a set of rules
governing the drama activities, providing the reason for them is
made clear, or providing they have a hand in their formulation.

If this is achieved by the teacher then the worry of what to do
next in drama will never arise. The skill which the teacher must
develop is that of quickly seeing the implications of every
suggestion and then to utilize them for the overall educational
purposes. This means being one step ahead and prepared
without restricting the possibilities for the children. The only
way to develop these skills is to get fully involved in the drama
and accept the risks.

No doubt mistakes will be made and the drama may at times
feel like a disaster area. If it appears to be getting nowhere then it
may have to be abandoned but if you try again and remember the

many control mechanisms available to the teacher, drama lessons will become, as I've found, not only enjoyable but exciting, and you will begin to bore the rest of the staff with stories of 'what happened today in drama'.

4 Development in a Drama Lesson—the Structure

Roles or identity; place or situation; focus or issue: which order?
In attempting to help children create a workable drama, you have to consider the three strands which combine to make the whole.

1 ROLES or Identity	2 PLACE or Situation	3 FOCUS or Issue
People	in a place	involved with others.
Who are you?	Where are you?	What are we concerned about?
A soldier	at a railway station	becoming anxious because of the lateness of the train.
A farmer	at a market	complaining to others of the price of fertilizer.
Pirates	on a ship	lost.

All three are necessary but it is not always easy to achieve a high level of commitment for each at all times. The question is, which one do you start with? I think it is wrong to expect all three to develop at the same rate, so it makes sense to concentrate at first on just one.

My inclination is to go for focus first and allow the roles to develop later in response to the focus. In the example of the circus, I took on a vague role but presented the children with a problem—How do you run a circus?—which they discussed with me in general terms, giving possible solutions. It was only when we came actually to get the circus going that particular roles became important. At first they were just a group of people, but when I asked 'Who knows about lions?' or 'Who can train horses?', the children began gradually to take roles. They decided what their roles were to be according to their interests or knowledge. Thus we had lion tamers, clowns, trapeze artists and tightrope walkers practising for opening night. If not too much pressure is put on at this stage, it is possible for the children to try out roles, discard them if necessary and try others. Gradually they will find the role for which they are most suited.

Up to this point, the sense of place will have been equally vague. 'Where are the Big Top, the lions' cages, the stables?' The answers to these questions were not important at the beginning but assume importance now that each person has a task.

If the situation is decided first, you might find that an area has been allocated to say, the seals, but no one fancies looking after the seals. Spatial divisions, therefore, especially if blocks or chairs are used, can restrict the development of the drama.

If I try the second approach, I ask a class to imagine that they are in a completely different place from their hall or classroom, I often get suggestions like jungles, the seaside, the moon, etc. The first piece of action must be to attempt to create in the children's minds this new environment. The place, therefore, dictates the course of the story. In the jungle, it is the trees, shrubs, swamps, rocks, and such. Everyone needs to know and agree as to where everything is and what particular problem it presents. However, you must retain some degree of flexibility or the action can never move away from that comparatively small area.

Having created an acceptable environment, you then need to change the emphasis of the question to people. 'Who are we?' and 'What are we doing here?'

The third line of approach is to concentrate on developing roles first. You ask the children 'Can you pretend to be another person?' You let them try out different types of people such as soldiers, hunters, nurses, kings and queens. Then ask them to choose. Depending on how they answer, I usually say 'How would you walk?' 'What might you be doing?' 'Would you be carrying anything?'

Your next task is to relate all this to a place where these various people might come together. Not an easy task. The best way is always to ask the children for suggestions. Likely responses are places where many various people might congregate such as airports, markets, railway stations and seaside resorts. Finding a focus can also be difficult although there will be no shortage of 'dramatic' suggestions like robberies, crashes, hi-jacks, earthquakes and volcanoes.

In the motorway development example (p. 47), the children first built up their roles and their village. Later I provided the focus by playing the role of the man from the developers who threatened the villagers' way of life.

Although identification with role and place is vitally important, I have always found that it is the focus (the problem or issue) that is the main determining factor. If you have a focus which really holds the interest of the class, the rest will take care of itself.

5 Using Various Stimuli to Start Drama

The best way to start drama is to sit down with the children and discuss what they would like to do. Often there will be a subject or topic arising from other work in the classroom which provides a suitable starting point. If nothing emerges from this method, then it might be necessary to provide some stimulus which will spark off ideas and set the children's creativity moving. We all get tired at times.

It is therefore a good idea to have a collection of useful starters ready for emergencies when ideas dry up. These could include stories, illustrations or objects.

Stories
There is no finer source of ideas than the school or classroom library. However, if story is to be the basis for drama, it must only be the bare bones with the flesh yet to be added. There must be ample elbow room to explore and invent. Acting out existing well-known stories has, I feel, only limited value. Effective drama is always about the behaviour of human beings in a state of tension or conflict. A 'What shall we do about . . .?' situation. The story must be used to suggest starting points, topics or themes. Hopefully, the drama will develop on its own tack leaving the original plot completely.

The start of the story might be read or told to a class and the drama begins when you ask 'I wonder what might happen next?' or 'If you were those people what would you do?' So the children enter the story halfway through. Here is an example:

'I was running through a forest one day, when suddenly I

tripped and fell. I looked to see what had caused me to trip, and I discovered a metal ring fixed to the ground. I wondered what it was doing in the middle of the forest, but I had no time to find out just then, but I was determined to return, and bring some helpers with me. Will you come with me and find out what it means?'

One incident from a story may be used as a basis. Talking of the story *Jack and the Beanstalk*, you might say 'Jack and his mother were so poor, they had to sell the cow, I wonder what else they might have tried first?' and so a drama about being poor is started.

One bonus from this method, if it is a new story, is that afterwards you can tell the class that the story they have just 'lived through' can be found in the library but with a difference.

Illustrations

Photographs or reproductions of paintings collected from magazines and colour supplements offer you, ready-made, one or more of the elements of a drama, not only people and places but also atmosphere.

Pictures of Places

Forests, deserts, underwater scenes, lunar landscapes, swamps, castles and other buildings or other exotic locations. It is often preferable that they are not too specific or obvious so that by subtle questioning, the children's imaginations will begin to work.

Example:

'Try to imagine that you are in the middle of this desert. What words can you think of to describe how you might feel? What would you see all round you? Close your eyes and imagine the hot sun beating down.' When the children are quiet, begin straight away. 'Does anyone know how many days we've been in this desert? Perhaps there has been a plane crash or the group is lost. How long will we last in this desert? How can we get help?'

Once the class has absorbed the atmosphere of the picture, and discussed its implications, you can put it on one side and their interpretations will take over.

Pictures of characters

Individuals engaged in their occupation or in the street, in special dress. These are easily available and evoke an atmosphere.

'Who is he?'

'What are they doing?'

Examples

a gypsy woman	an explorer	a railway worker
a sailor	a bedouin	a cowboy
a factory worker	an old person	

Pictures of large groups of people in their setting

a farm	an airport	a market
a store	the seaside	a race meeting
a factory	an office	

Pictures of people in conflict or in difficulties

| a demonstration | a strike | on a ship in a storm |
| a war picture | vandals | |

People in an argument or conflict because of their differences

| explorers and tribesmen | workers and management | police and rioters |

The pictures are only a means to attract the children's attention and provide a focus from which discussion can start. As soon as ideas begin to flow, the picture can be discarded. One or two elements may be in the picture but the situation needs to be narrowed down before the drama can start and that requires skilful questioning. You must make it clear whether the picture is offered to spark off ideas or as a means of helping the children into a situation you would like them to explore. With a picture of a polar region you might ask:

'Who or what might live or have lived in such a land?'

'Who might want to journey through such a land?'
With a picture of a person, you might ask:
'Why do you think they are looking like that?'
'Would you like to be there?'
'What would you say if you met him?'
The purpose of the questions is not to test their observation powers but to arouse their interest. It is to move from a broad stimulus which offers many possibilities to a specific and selected situation which the children can begin to enter, to become part of and live through. You must resist the temptation to ask too many questions and to over-define the situation, stopping at the point when enough is known to make a start. Often it pays in the questioning to concentrate on one aspect of the topic, such as the task which people in the picture are engaged in:
'What jobs would you be doing?'
or the mood of the people:
'What would they be feeling at that time?'
'What are they waiting for?'
'Are they going to change their minds?'

Artefacts
Objects are doubly useful because they can not only help to start off drama by being a stimulus but they can be actually used as part of the action, being felt and handled as well as seen. A well-chosen object including part of a costume can help to add reality to the imagined situation. A piece of bright cloth draped across a chair to make a more convincing throne. A lantern whose light we must avoid if we are to escape. Moreover, an object can be not merely a property, but a symbol. The great key which hangs from the jailor's belt, the crown, the sword, the flag, and bowl can mean far more than their usefulness.

The object may simply be shown to the class at the beginning or given to a child to feel.

'Who would use this?'   'Where did you find it?'
'What could it be used for?'   'What does it mean?'

It is a good idea to collect unusual objects which have many uses and meanings. Objects from another age or country which are not too specific are particularly valuable.

Another approach is to use the object in a role.

Examples
Writing with a quill pen.
Looking through a telescope.
Pouring a liquid into a jar.
Holding a skull.
Reading a scroll.

Success still depends on using questions to allow the children to create the scenario. Do not start with a fixed idea of what you think it should mean. If you do that you will probably be disappointed or you will succeed in frustrating the children's creativity.

Remember these are only starting points not *plots*.

Example: FLAGS.
One day I was met at the school gates by a little boy who presented me with a long black pole on which was a 'Skull and Cross Bones' flag. He said, 'My Mam made this for you to do drama.'

It was obvious that I had to use this flag as a starting point.

It had been arranged that I should take two sessions with different age groups, so I decided to use the flag with both, to see whether the response would be different. When I showed the flag to the children, it was, of course, quickly recognized. 'Does this flag mean the same to everyone who sees it?' I asked. The reply which came was 'Depends on whether you are a pirate or not.' Then another child said, 'If you are a pirate, it makes you feel *brave*. If not, it makes you feel *scared*.'

The younger children wanted to be pirates but the older ones favoured meeting pirates, so from the same stimulus came a completely different drama.

6 Teacher in Role

Opportunities offered: types of role available

When some teachers attempt to involve themselves in children's drama, they make the mistake of remaining the teacher or a teacher-like figure who gives orders, asks questions all the time but really knows the answers. It comes as no surprise to be told by teachers that the effect they have on Wendy house type play is that it stops or the children become embarrassed or stand and wait for instructions. Teaching in role offers the opportunity to become fully involved without being teacher. This new teacher which the children see is one who can sometimes be wrong; who does not know all the answers; who may be questioned, criticized, excluded, challenged, and even ignored. But also a teacher who listens, asks for advice, needs help, seeks reassurance, and thinks your ideas might be important.

Obviously children know that you are still their teacher but they will soon recognize that you are being 'someone else' for a time as long as they know why. If they are given the chance to discuss what is happening or what has happened, they will quickly appreciate the reasons. There is no place for con tricks or deceit. You simply say, 'I am now going to be another person, you will be able to tell who I am by the way I talk and what I say.' When you start in role like this, you must carefully observe the effect you are having. Are they accepting you in role or are they still seeing teacher? Are they giggling or looking afraid? If you are not sure, the best course is to stop, become teacher again and ask the children why they responded as they did. 'Did you find it funny?' 'Was I like a real person?' 'Were you scared?'

Then you might say, 'Now you know what to expect, shall we try again?' Before any progress can be made, you must be sure they understand and are ready to accept you 'in role'. It may be necessary to come out of role many times during a session in the same way as the children will come in and out of their roles many times. A short period when they reflect on their roles is usually very valuable. They will obviously still come to you when they want to go to the toilet or if they are not feeling too well. You are still there if they need you.

You are still the teacher if you have to be, but teaching in role, I believe, allows you to do your job more effectively. It multiplies the number of options available.

When you use a role, you gain another person (another adult) to respond to the call:

'What are you doing in my field?'

Another life-style comes into the room:

'The servants in this household bow when her ladyship enters, is that clear?'

This other person provides a focus to enquire into:

'Who is she?' 'What does she want?'

Or a specific example (a personification) of a challenge to beliefs and assumptions, e.g. The lonely witch, the timid dragon.

The role can be used to teach facts and attitudes, pose questions, demand understanding.

'Do you have to be cruel to train animals to do tricks?'

You can be aggressive or can support the minority view or present alternatives.

'If you have to be cruel then I'm not having animals in my circus.'

'They said we should call the police.'

'I always thought that you had to . . .'

'I once read that . . .'

'Is that the only way to . . .'

'If we make that sort of noise, the pirates will hear us and we'll all be dead.'

'And I don't want any dead heroes.'

To use role effectively, you must be clear in your mind as to what effect you want to create, what pressure to exert and how the role will do this. Will it be by voice, stance or by the use of some symbolic 'prop'? (e.g. baton, walking stick, spear, bucket). It is important, at first, to take on very low-key roles avoiding amateur dramatics, not too strong but clearly defined without being fixed. If you are to move in and out of role, the children must know when you have changed. Usually a symbolic action can be used to demonstrate that the transformation has taken place. This signal also indicates when the children also are to come out of role, at least temporarily. It could simply be a case of moving over to a particular corner of the room, sitting on a certain chair or even using a sound. I often start drama off by saying 'When I click my fingers, we are. . . .' 'Are you ready?' I have seen other teachers using a cymbal or tambourine or drum for the same effect.

Besides moving in and out of role, you can also change roles if the original role has served its purpose and another appears to offer more opportunities. Your role could be assumed by another member of the class or quietly allowed to be played out of the drama.

Remember your function in a drama lesson is to challenge, accuse, interest, threaten, make anxious, or give confidence. You are concerned with creating areas of learning. In any one lesson, you need to operate in one or more of the following ways:

challenger	apprentice	dictator
listener	servant	guide
arbiter	dim-wit	Devil's advocate
coward	comforter	critic
co-ordinator		

When you play a role, the children are encouraged to take responsibility for what happens, freed from the restraint of getting the wrong answer. It is for you to say,

'I'm not going down there, it is too dangerous.'
'You had better make up your mind or else.'
'I don't know . . .'
'Are you sure?'

One very important objective at the beginning of the drama session or with children who are new to drama, is to keep the group together responding to one focal stimulus. Nothing is more effective than teacher taking on the role of a person in need of help, information or expertise. This type of role effectively reverses the normal classroom role system by turning the children into the experts.

Another successful type of role is the agent, the person who is only carrying out orders or limited in his powers. Because he/she is acting for someone else, he/she cannot bear full responsibility for unpleasant decisions. 'It's not my fault.' 'I agree with you but he's the boss.'

The class are thus united not against you but with you. You can act as co-ordinator controlling the structure of the action but not the content or ideas. In role as the owner of the circus which I had been left in my uncle's will, I knew nothing about running a circus except that it had to be good and make money or I would sell it and all the employees would be out of a job. The children were the experts (lion tamers, trapeze artists, etc). I could insist on high quality work on the basis of my ignorance.

'Do you think that will work?'

'This doesn't strike me as particularly efficient.'

'It doesn't make me laugh.'

Another useful role is that of the 'stranger'. This enables you to get the children to explain who they are and what they are doing.

In a market situation—you could be a government health inspector. Or in the Nativity—Caesar's envoy:

'What has been going on here?'

'I've heard a new king has been born, what do you know about it?'

Or a reporter getting the facts straight:

'Could you tell me . . .?'

'Is it true . . .?'

Again you start from the position of complete ignorance but because you have to write a report you have to get at the truth. You can question, cross-question, challenge, call witnesses, criticize or accuse. The keynote is scepticism.

In the motorway development example (p. 47), I was the stranger at first but later revealed myself as the villain. This role could have been played so that the whole class would have united against me, but this would not have served my purpose at that moment. With a new class, uniting the children against is not advisable. I, therefore, played the role with a smile, firmly believing that I was offering them a new Jerusalem and being surprised that they were not more grateful. For some members of the village, I was able to offer jobs and other inducements which they could not refuse so they became my supporters and accomplices. The discussion about the relative merits of the scheme was then carried on among various groups with the 'stranger' as onlooker.

Sometimes the best role is one allowing for maximum flexibility because it is so vague. I have often been asked by observers what my role was when I had waited to intervene if necessary but the need had not arisen. If the drama is going well and focusing on important learning areas, it is unwise to show your hand too early. Often your best strategy might be to quietly move around, responding to individual children's actions or remarks. Sometimes I have found myself playing different roles with different groups of children.

Whatever role you assume, remember that your main aim is to promote the experience and elevate it, not merely to go along the same road as the children. You must be able to take trivial contributions and make them significant so that the drama is raised to a higher plane of experience.

7 The Content of Drama— Using Topics

Never underestimate young children
I believe that primary children are capable of responding to quite demanding creative and intellectual stimuli. Only if this is done, will really good drama follow.

Too often children are allowed to get away with the superficial by only being provided with opportunities for acting stories they already know, or merely repeating activities that they do quite adequately without the teacher, in their own time.

Of course, use their fantasy world and their natural ability to play, but this must be structured so that they are faced with a new challenge. It is the teacher's job to provide the focus, which gives the drama direction. Doing a 'circus' is a common theme, but what prevents this from being merely play-acting or a movement exercise is, for example, the question—'How do you train animals to do tricks?' or 'Why is the clown so unhappy?'

What to do in drama—using a topic or story
If children suggest 'witches' as a subject for drama, many teachers tend instinctively to think of the witch in *Hansel and Gretel* or Macbeth's witches. In other words, they think in terms of established stories. By doing this, which is fairly natural, they have already limited, very severely, the scope of the drama. If 'witches' is suggested you must be asking yourself 'What do they mean by witches?' 'What particular aspect of witches attracts or interests them?' 'What are the implications behind the suggestions?' 'Is it that witches are evil or that they have magic powers?' 'Do they want to be witches or to meet a witch?' You

could proceed by saying: 'Tell me about witches?' or 'How do you become a witch?' or 'What would you say to a witch?' or 'Are witches people?' Most children will tell you that witches wear black clothes, have long noses, are ugly, that they use cauldrons and make spells, and have broomsticks. But how many would say that witches are lonely or have laws or were persecuted?

Good drama will come from avoiding or veering away from the familiar caricature, the superficial. The aim is to see the witch as an individual not a stereotype. 'Can you have a good witch?' 'How could you get a witch to help you?' 'Could we learn to be witches?' 'Would you invite a witch to a party?'

'Doing witches' must help the children to see something new, a new insight into some aspect of life. 'How do you make friends with a witch?' is really about making friends with somebody who appears aggressive and unfriendly, perhaps the old and lonely. 'Witches' also could be about good and evil or coming to terms with fear.

Virtually any subject is possible: TV and film themes, nursery rhymes, fairy stories, myths and legends can all be used, but the problem is finding the focus and a starting point. This must be something which they can immediately recognize, e.g. being happy, sad or angry. I always find successful the apparently incongruous or the paradoxical, such as:

   the friendly ghost
   the gentle giant
   the reluctant dragon
   the unhappy princess (prince, king, etc)
   the soft pirates
   the Viking who was always seasick
   the gardener without green fingers
   the monster without a friend
   the homesick Martians
   the incompetent witch

In all of these, there is someone who needs help, and appeals to the children. Any number of good situations can start with the expression of some need: 'Can you help me?'—

'I've lost my dog.'
'Do you know anything about castles?'
'I must get some more animals for my zoo.'
'My house is in a terrible mess!'
'Will you come with me?'
'The treasure is hidden here somewhere!'
'Have you ever climbed a mountain?'
'How do you catch a monster?'
'Can you keep a secret?'
'None of my spells work!'

The problems should never be such as can easily be solved with technical knowledge, but those which are universal to all ages and abilities. 'How do you make a person happy?' or 'How do you give a person confidence?' or 'How can we trust him?' There are no ready answers to questions of this sort; teachers and pupils are on equal terms. In this way the children are 'upgraded' by paying the role of the experts. They draw on their inner resources, and experience as a group, in order to reach a decision or solve a problem.

Some ideas on using well-known stories

The Nativity
1. Ask the class to imagine that they are residents of Nazareth. What are their houses like? What are they doing?
You then be the messenger and read the proclamation.
2. Be the Innkeeper, the children are incoming travellers. 'Sorry we've no room left.'
3. In small groups or pairs, the class recall the story for their grandchildren years later.

Guy Fawkes
1. The class as conspirators creep about along the side streets at night, afraid of being seen and then arrive at the secret meeting place.
'How do we know whom we can trust?' 'How can we kill the

King and all our enemies?' 'Anyone know anything about gunpowder?'
2. You be a King's agent.
'We have Guy Fawkes, so now we want his accomplices. Where were you on the night of November 5th?'

Moses
1. 'Why would anyone want to kill a baby?'
2. 'You take the risk of trusting me or remain as slaves.'

Ali Baba
1. As the thieves.
'Are you sure nobody will ever find our treasure here?' 'Who will be our leader?' 'How do we share out the treasure?'
2. As others who find the cave.
'How do we get out of here without being caught by the thieves?' 'If we take the treasure, shall we keep it or give it back to its rightful owners?'

Pied Piper
1. Before the Pied Piper arrives:
'What can we do about these rats, has anyone got any suggestions?'
2. Later:
'How can we get our children back?'
3. Be the Mayor.
'Now we have got rid of the rats, we don't need to worry.'
4. Be the Piper.
'I want my money.'

Jack and the Beanstalk
1. Revisit the Giant's Castle.
'How do we get there without a Beanstalk?' 'Is the Giant really dead?'
2. Be the Giant's wife.
'Who are you people? What do you want?'

Sleeping Beauty
1. 'How can we make sure the princess never pricks her finger?'
2. Be the bad fairy with the children trying to persuade you to cancel your spell.

Noah and the Flood
1. Be Noah trying to convince the people that there is to be a flood.
2. Be the main doubter.
3. The children could be Noah's family designing and then building the Ark, 'Big enough to take all those animals.'
4. 'Where are we going to get the food for all these animals?' 'What does an ostrich eat?'

Robin Hood
1. Be outlaws.
'Where shall we build our hide-out?'
'How can we rescue our men?'
2. Be the Sheriff or one of his henchmen.
Questioning villagers.
'Where can I find Robin Hood? Tell me or . . .'
Collecting taxes.
'Pay or we burn your house.'

Approaches to work situations

Supermarket or chainstore
'How can we stop shop-lifters?' 'We must sell more or we go bust.'
You could be the Manager, Store Detective or Hygiene Inspector.

Zoo or circus
'How do you get animals to do tricks?' 'What do giraffes eat?' 'Is it cruel?' 'Not enough people are coming in the turnstiles, how can we attract more?'

Fire station
'Are we quick enough?' 'How can we prevent fires?'

Bank
Running a bank and checking security or a gang planning a robbery.

Station
'Why is the train always late?'

Airport
Lost luggage. Fog. Hi-jack. Plane crash. Strike.

Hospital
'Besides doctors and nurses, are there any other people who work in a hospital?'

Planning or designing

Playground
The children as experts are asked to design a children's playground.
'What would you really like?'
You be the man from the Council.
'I don't think we can afford that.'

Village
The children design and build a village for children only.

Church
Is this a special church?
Preparing the church for a special event—a wedding or coronation.

Castle
You be the king's steward, the children the expert designers and builders.
'The king commands you to build the finest castle in England.'

Other examples

a stately home	a new housing estate	a newspaper
a school	a building site	a barracks
a prison	a garage	a fairground
a farm	a factory	

The 'Flash Gordon' principle

Obtaining a high level of commitment to a drama takes time. Sometimes for a class to become really involved in their roles and the situation can take a whole session. If you attempt to start a new topic every time, you run the risk of never getting beyond the obvious and superficial. I have, therefore, come to believe in the 'Flash Gordon' principle.

When I used to go to the children's Saturday cinema, the programme was always composed of a number of weekly serials. At the end of each film, the hero was usually facing death or disaster. Flash Gordon, my favourite, was about to be crushed to death or thrown into the villain's snake-pit. The suspense was such that you had to come back the following week to discover their fate. And, of course, these films were designed for just that purpose.

Now if you have regular sessions of drama, you would like the children to arrive ready and eager each time so you can start immediately without any time being wasted in preparations. Adopting the 'Flash Gordon' principle means making sure each drama session ends on a high note, a crucial moment, so when the children arrive for the next session they are raring to go. For example, the point to stop is when the pirates appear on the horizon or when you've just found the treasure or you've been shipwrecked. In each case, the next session starts with an exciting question: 'What are we going to do about the pirates?' 'Where are we going to hide the treasure?' 'How are we going to survive on this island?'

In my view, it is not necessary to tie up all the loose ends. The story does not need to end each time. The children should go away thinking, trying to discover answers to the questions facing them in the drama. A session about farming ended up with the children trying to discover how to get the chickens to start laying eggs. Children will use the intervening period to 'research' into the topic, looking through books in the library or asking their parents. One little boy returned to tell me that to get chickens to lay eggs, you use a ceramic egg so that they pick up the idea. I still do not believe it but I have been assured that it works.

Lesson example—the motorway
The children had spent some time building up the idea of an idyllic village, 'beautiful old-fashioned houses with pretty gardens.' I took on the role of a complete stranger asking questions about the village, taking notes and photographs. Because of my interest, the inhabitants were pleased to provide me with all the information needed. They made a large map of the village and drew pictures of their cottages which were inserted onto this map.

I thanked them for all their help and kindness but then revealed that their village had been specially chosen for a new development connected with the motorway. I proceeded to outline all the benefits which will accrue to the village as a result of these changes.

The villagers were informed that a public meeting was to be held where their views would be heard and any questions answered. In the meantime, no doubt they had a lot to discuss. The class split up into groups to consider the proposals and plan further action. In my role of 'stranger' I took this opportunity to speak to the small groups, one by one, attempting to create dissension by obtaining some support for the development idea. I also spoke to individuals offering inducements, special contracts, jobs, etc.

When we held the public meeting, the villagers were not as united as they had been earlier. Instead of the arguments raging with the stranger, 'the bad guy', fierce disputes broke out between the inhabitants with the stranger really acting as chairman. This occurred as a result of being told that they would have to decide by a majority vote.

Analysis

This was a single but fairly long sesson which started in the hall and was continued in the classroom. At all times 'the stranger' was pleasant, courteous and appeared genuinely to want to do the best for the village. Their opposition to him later was based on their commitment to their village which had been built up in the early part of the session. The 'stranger' role helped to reinforce this attachment. The challenge that came with the presentation of the plan never became a personal challenge but was concerned with the ideas.

8 Control and Discipline in Drama Lessons

How to avoid chaos

Many teachers do not attempt drama because they are afraid of possible discipline problems. They see drama as offering too much freedom for the children to get out of hand. Yet good discipline in drama is essential. If there is a lack of control, the value of the activity is lost. What is done will be very superficial and really a waste of time. The children will either be messing about or merely doing what they can do just as well in the playground. Good drama demands full commitment and concentration. I constantly claim that children can work harder in drama than in any other lesson. My aim is always to ensure that they think more deeply and for longer. This cannot be done without an atmosphere of order and control.

A silent class sitting behind desks engaged in writing is perhaps the ideal for many teachers. This can occur during drama lessons but only occasionally will it be appropriate. All too often teachers start drama by taking the class into the hall and telling the children to spread out or 'find a space'. Both, I believe, are mistakes. By doing this they lose that vital close contact with the children. If you wish to be cautious, start the lesson in the classroom with the children behind desks or sitting on the floor around you as they do during story time. Concentrate on simple whole group problem-solving with little or no movement but basic role play. As an example, I once asked a class whether they were any good at making people happy. When they assured me that they were, I told the story of the sad king (princess, etc). I asked the children would they be the special people who had been sent for to help. If you try this sort of thing you could either be the king or perhaps be one of those people as well. 'Can you help me?' or 'How can we help the king?'

What you are aiming for at this stage is first, interest and secondly, commitment to solving the problem in verbal terms. You could find a new angle to a well-known story by pretending to be one of the characters. Be one of the ugly sisters and say something like, 'It's not fair what happened to Cinderella, she gets all the luck' or 'Has that nuisance of a sister been telling stories about me. What has she told you?'

You will get a fairly lively response to this because they already know the story so well and you can rephrase any question to cater for the responses you receive. Doing this with one class, the situation resolved into the question of whether fairy godmothers actually existed and if so have I got one?

Sometimes I have asked each member of the class to think up the answer to a particular problem and put it down on paper in written or picture form. The problem could be to design a children's playground, the wedding dress for a princess or my new house. This they do back at their desks where you would expect quiet concentration. For the children's playground example, the class were the experts called in by the council and I was the man from the council. When they returned to sit around me in the reading corner every child was asked to describe their idea (if they could) and each paper was stuck on the wall for all to see. Thus the class could see that not only were they being asked to work but that their work was being given a special kind of attention. They were being made to feel important, their ideas listened to by the teacher (in role) and by the rest of the class, and that the task had a purpose (i.e. it was not just to please teacher).

In a drama discussion, the aim is not only to have child to teacher and teacher to child interactions but also child to child interactions with teacher acting as chairman. Discussions with young children can, at times, be rather chaotic at first. They, of course, all want equal attention, they all talk at once and do little listening to each other. Whole class discussions, therefore, must be fairly short.

Child to child discussions can be encouraged by structuring the problem-solving in pairs or later in fours. When you call them back, however, it is very important to check on what they have been doing. Have they found a solution? What is the decision of their group? Make it clear you expect a decision otherwise they might chatter away about anything. They must feel that it is important to themselves and to the story. Insist on some response.

If the story appears to demand space, it may be possible now to consider moving some of the chairs and tables to one side. I often ask each group to elect a spokesman so that when you recall the groups together you ask this elected person to explain or describe their idea to the rest of the class. Every suggestion (and now there will not be so many) must be given full attention from all, carefully considered and discussed. 'Will it work?' 'Which idea shall we try first?'

No idea must be dismissed or ridiculed (however stupid) if it has been arrived at seriously and honestly. The suggestion in the example described earlier (of the journey into space going to the sun) was almost laughed at by the class but later led to building our rocket of asbestos.

The most effective control on children operating in this new way will be your attitude to the work. If you approach the drama with seriousness and commitment, the class will do the same.

After trying these methods, you might now decide to use the hall and take advantage of the extra space. If so, certain questions need to be asked of yourself. How much space do you actually need? And for what purpose? Primary school halls are unfortunately often corridors, store rooms and are adjacent to the school kitchen. I have experienced attempting to do drama with a class accompanied by Radio One and non-stop gossip, banging and clanging from the dinner ladies. These are not the most ideal conditions for serious concentration.

One primary school headteacher I know placed a notice on the hall door which said:

DRAMA IN PROGRESS—NO INTERRUPTIONS

This was made clear to all the children, the rest of the staff, dinner ladies and caretaker. This particular headteacher, while she was doing drama, refused to answer the telephone, no matter who the caller was.

It must then be made clear to the children where drama *can* and *cannot* take place, e.g. not on the PE apparatus, under the dining tables or behind the piano. They must learn what can be used, e.g. rostra blocks and what may be dangerous. In one hall I marked out the area for drama with yellow tape. The headteacher I mentioned earlier used to talk to the children about the hall being 'the magic room' but always reminded them at the beginning of each session of the rules by asking 'But where does the magic stop?', referring to the climbing frames, cupboards, tables, etc. If this is not made clear to children at the start, drama becomes impossible if not dangerous.

It is often a good idea to have a teacher/class area. I have seen one teacher who says to her children, 'If I go and sit on this chair, I want you all to come and sit on the floor around me.' She then practises this until she is sure they fully understand. This acting symbolically tells the class that they are to come out of their drama and that their teacher is teacher again. Other teachers use a drum or tambourine for the same purpose.

Too much space can ruin drama. If you are not careful, the children will associate the activity with movement or PE and concentrate on actions rather than ideas. If you want the class to work in groups as in the classroom, allocate them a particular place to work and insist that they remain in that space. Make sure no one starts running around the hall interfering with others. If necessary mark out the areas with chalk. One class I worked with was building a large house. The children had divided themselves into groups, each responsible for different parts of the house. At first I drew a plan of the house on the blackboard. This we transferred onto the floor of the hall. The groups then moved into their areas to work, knowing not only their own space but also where everyone else was working. If a worker encroached on another's area, this was immediately reported to the owner (i.e. me). With some other children running a circus, the issue became the control of the animals who had a tendency to wander. It was important to the drama to have clearly delineated areas and this was appreciated by all the class.

These early sessions are partly concerned with learning the medium of drama, the same way that children doing pottery for the first time have to learn the characteristics of clay. What you can and cannot do. Drama should be seen in the same way. If it has been decided that the room is a forest, then it is a forest. A second later it can be a swamp or a castle. If you need to climb a tree, you imagine the tree is there. You do not need to climb the wall bars or on top of the piano. There is no need to pile up chairs or tables. To hide, you again do not need to go behind the dinner tables or in the PE store.

The principle of agreeing to pretend implies a sensitivity to others and a consideration for their imaginary world. What is involved is the discipline of mutual acceptance. Drama is nothing if it is not a co-operative group activity; children learning to work together in a common task to a common end.

The most crucial factor in maintaining order and control, if this is a problem, is the role the teacher takes. To maintain credibility, you must be part of the drama, i.e. be in the forest or on a mountain with the children. You can only influence events if you are there as well. Otherwise all you do is interrupt or stop the story. Interventions from outside the drama can quickly destroy the commitment and involvement that you have been working for. Very soon the children will either begin to get bored, mess about or will meekly wait to be told what to do. If you are a participant, your interventions become an integral part of the story. The role will legitimately allow you to maintain control. You can stop or slow down the action, question the group, challenge decisions, throw doubt on their methods or actions. 'Do you think this will work?' 'What will happen if they hear us?' or more aggressively 'Keep your head down or we're all in trouble.' You are not making decisions or providing the information but you are making the children see the implications of their actions. In the example of the circus, I was the owner but not the expert. I could call meetings and cross-examine the experts. I could praise or admonish. I could be angry or very pleased not as teacher but in the role of owner.

After a session, I often ask a class about the role I took. I ask, 'Did you like him?' 'Did you trust him?' or 'Do you think that people like that really exist?' By doing this, the children see the other person as distinct from the teacher and appreciate the significance of your role in relation to their own.

9 Some Problems— Help

These are questions which I have been often asked by teachers who have been attempting to do drama.

What do you do about the loner?
All the children must be given the opportunity to join in when they are ready. They must be allowed to make up their own minds. Allow them to watch at first. Do not pressurize them to become involved too early or they will be put off for good. In other words, keep an eye on them but appear to ignore them publicly. If they look ready but perhaps are afraid or do not know, seize the opportunity to involve them very gently with you in role with a question like 'Have you seen anyone selling oranges?' or 'It's a good market this, have you been before?'—not too threatening. If you feel they could be ready to join in, you can either get them to help you or use one of their friends.

'Could you help me to set up my stall?' or 'I am the market manager, could you help me inspect the stalls?'

Using a friend, you might say,'They are so busy on that stall today, could you help them?' or alternatively get the friend to come over to issue the invitation.

A common mistake is to expect full and complete involvement of all children at the same rate. Give them time. They must feel secure in a new medium. Some children throw themselves into any activity with lots of movement and noise. They are the ones who want to answer all the questions and take the lead. Others are far more passive in their involvement. The real action is taking place in their heads as it should be. Always remember that drama is not a movement lesson. Do not go for good acting or 'miming' in the stage sense. Good drama is a combination of the cerebral and the emotional. If a child does not appear to be doing very much, the way to find out if they are with you or not, is either to talk to them in role or ask a question (in private). The response will reveal all. They may be just watching you or the other children and waiting for an opportunity. They may not be sure of what is expected of them or what role to take or what task to embark on. The worst way is to tell them what you think they should do.

What about the bright active leaders?
In the usual very mixed primary class, there will be a wide range of ability, interests and degrees of maturity. It is always difficult to find the correct level. Even if you yourself try to direct the action, you risk either making it too easy or too hard. It is important to provide the children with challenges that are so universal that they can be faced up to at many different levels whether they work in groups or as individuals. A class, for example, running a circus can meet with endless challenges, ranging from the simplest task to some fundamental and very real problems. One child may quite happily clean down the elephants and take great pride in this; another designs a poster; while another teaches the seals to do tricks. During this period you can move about the area questioning, helping, challenging, acting as a link between groups and sharing problems. E.g. 'We have a problem over here. Does anyone know how you weigh an elephant?'

In every situation, there will be some more demanding tasks or problems. There will be a need for people with special skills and expertise. Moreover, there will be a need for leaders. All of this enables you to provide suitable roles or tasks to the bright active members of the class.

Children come to schools at varying stages of understanding and degrees of social responsiveness. While the majority adapt readily to social demands, others retain strong egocentric tendencies until they are six or even seven. Consequently bringing young children together in group drama activities requires a framework offering security and confidence and one that can cope with differences as well as provide opportunities for creative endeavour. But most older children are capable of reaching the stage where they actively help to build and shape their drama, discuss events and issues within it and respond to the challenge of having problems to solve. This capacity seems to be developed most where drama allows children a share of responsibility. It is a process marked by trust, exercise of choice, opportunity to try out ideas and the chance to make mistakes in safety.

Drama increases the need for children to work together and in turn the drama itself gains from children developing group awareness, sense of responsibility and commitment. The teacher's task is to use the medium of drama to provide learning experiences for children on the principle that what children care about most they will learn best. Thus the role of the teacher is to enable, to give responsibility to the learner but at the same time to manipulate the potential of the dramatic medium in such a way as to focus on learning areas for the child.

What do you do to make them listen?
Basically children will listen intently and follow what is said only if they are interested or feel that there is something in it for them. It is relatively easy to get a class quiet and looking at you while you speak. That does not necessarily mean that they are listening. The only way to be sure is to ask questions. But when you do this you then have the problem of who answers first and whether they will listen to each other. Getting the right answer and receiving praise is normally the motivation. In this, the rest of the class are competitors not collaborators. The way drama influences this is by altering the social interactional structure of the group from being teacher and thirty or so individuals to a single group with a common aim and problem. No one person asks all the questions or provides all the information. In whatever role you take you will probably still be asking questions but they will not be teacher questions but real questions arising

from the situation. E.g. 'What do we do now?' 'How do we get out?'

At first the children will still feel that there is a right answer so they will put up their hands and try to please teacher by guessing what is in her/his mind. Those who do not might fidget, chatter amongst themselves or generally mess about. It has to be made very clear that what is required is their opinion and everybody will be heard. You may need to repeat these suggestions and write them on a blackboard so everyone can see. Then ask which do they agree with or which will work. Give each answer equal attention no matter how inappropriate it might appear. Try not to show your preferences—be the impartial chairman. Then insist that they decide. Ask for comments and opinions. Constantly bounce these back to the children especially to those who might appear not to be fully involved. 'What do you think?' Have rules and insist on everyone commiting themselves. Divide the class into groups with the specific task of coming to a conclusion. Ensure that the whole class is fully aware of the implications of any decisions that are made. If this becomes the pattern for your lessons, then very soon all the class will listen both to you and to each other because they want to and feel it is important.

I haven't the confidence to slow down the action. What can I do?
Children left to themselves would run through *War and Peace, Ben Hur* and all the stories of the Brothers Grimm in five minutes flat. This is often the problem with known-story-based drama. The children want to rush to the action without considering any of the implications of that action. If this happens regularly you are wasting your time and theirs. Your role as teacher is to make the children stop and think because therein lies the educational value. The best way to achieve this is to concentrate on one focus at a time so that the children are so wrapped up in dealing with the problem before them that they do not see a story as such until the end when they might look back.

In the example of the 'Unhappy King' the children were trying to help him, the only obvious end being the king suddenly starting to smile. In the role of king, I was not going to allow this to occur until I felt they had earned it. The secret of slowing down the action is not to allow the chidren to project too far ahead. Each situation must be made a sufficient stumbling block so that it cannot be too easily overcome or side-stepped, e.g. do not allow members of a Stone-age tribe to suddenly produce dynamite or helicopters. It is equally important not to make the problem so difficult that they despair and get bored. When you see this happening, that's the moment to allow the easy solution and you move on.

When a group of children with whom I was working, wanted to charge into this cave, I used my role as 'coward' to slow the action. 'I'm not going in there to get killed'.

Another technique is to add a little information which stops them in their tracks. 'I once heard that . . .' or 'What are we going to do about . . .?' or 'How do we know the witch won't put a spell on us?' or 'What sort of air will we find?'

Another idea is *The Inspection:* 'I don't want to find anyone dead in the morning because of something silly like not knowing how to put up a tent, so stand next to your tents while I inspect. Nobody sleeps until I'm satisfied—is that clear?'

Another is *The Demonstration:* Here you use a group of children as the experts to demonstrate or explain what should be done, followed perhaps by a discussion or an inspection later by this special group.

Another is *The Ritual:* In this, every member of the class goes through a simple symbolic ritual which is compulsory. This could be signing on, bowing to the king, stirring the stew or some very dramatic ritual with full pomp and ceremony.

What do you do when children laugh and do not take seriously other children's involvement?
Children, we know, can be very cruel. They will, however, only laugh or jeer if it is somehow accepted to poke fun at others. If this is the case then it is up to you to show disapproval by giving full attention to all contributions. If later an idea is rejected it must be made clear that the child is not rejected also. One must try to create an atmosphere where no one is ever afraid to speak

up and make suggestions. If laughing persists it is, therefore, important to stop and discuss with the children why you are doing drama and to have constant reflection on what has happened. It must be made clear that it is a serious activity and is *work* even if in a very pleasurable form.

Moreover, by taking on a role yourself, you are legitimizing the activity. 'If teacher does it, it must be all right.' If you take it seriously, very soon so will all the others.

What do you do when children resent the fact that their particular idea has not been used?

I usually find that the big problem, once children get used to drama, is that you have to cope with too many ideas and that everyone feels that their idea is the best. Drama has its own rules but it is primarily a social activity. In fact, many teachers use drama in their teaching because it is such a valuable means of developing amongst children various social skills. It is not that children need these skills as pre-requisites for drama but that drama activities encourage the development of good social habits and improve the social health of the whole class. Many egocentric children coming from a home where they could expect the full and undivided attention of mother (and/or father) naturally expect the same from teacher. They do not appreciate why this should not always be possible. A child who offers an idea wants to be listened to and given due attention. Even if you have twenty ideas this must still be the case. Which idea is taken up, should really be decided by the whole class, not you.

If you ask, 'What shall we do drama about?' and you get many diverse answers, make a list, discuss each one. Try out each idea with some movement so as to narrow down the options. 'Which one of these do you fancy?'

If you still have too many ideas, choose the top one and promise the children that next time they will do the others, one by one. Put these ideas in a prominent place in the classroom or hall and carry out the promise. On the whole, if children come to really enjoy drama—as they will—they will come to realize that concessions that benefit the drama are for their sake and the rest of the class.

What do you do when children keep changing roles so often that the drama is becoming rather superficial?
It is usually a mistake for roles to become fixed too soon—that is, before the drama has crystallized. Many children will find that the role they thought was right for them is irrelevant to the situation as a whole or does not involve or interest them any more. It is much better to allow children gradually to take on roles which seem to be important, both to them personally and to the context of the drama.

If they are constantly changing roles, it may be that they have not thought deeply enough about the implications of their roles and it is something they cannot cope with. If this becomes a big problem then time must be given to examine who or what they are, what they should wear, how they should walk, what tools they might use, what sort of life would they lead.

Get each child to talk to another about their role. Ask them to draw a picture of themselves in role, perhaps doing different tasks. This could be done in comic form or as part of a booklet called 'The Life of . . .' I have asked children to write letters to friends explaining what has been happening. I have taken on the role of television or radio reporter and then interviewed each character about the events. 'What did you find when you went into the cellars below Parliament?' or 'What exactly is a Fairy Godmother?' One class produced a large mural of the situation showing each person engaged in part of the action.

The main point of all this is to make the children feel that their role is important to the whole and therefore, is worthy of their attention. It must be said, however, that roles do sometimes work themselves out and do become redundant. Children must be helped to choose new roles if this is difficult for them but on the whole, the main principle must be for the children to be fully involved in constructing their own drama within their own interests, knowledge and capabilities.

10 Looking Ahead

This book was written in response to specific questions from teachers who wished to do drama with their children but were put off by the practical problems.

Once you have overcome these initial difficulties, however, and your drama sessions begin to take off, the scope is endless. There are schools where drama dominates the whole school curriculum; where drama-based projects last from one term to the next; where children create a role over a long period and live in that role for a full term, receiving and writing letters, buying and selling land and houses, living through one reign to another, experiencing life in a completely different community in another country or age.

All this becomes possible when you and your children feel secure in what you are doing and understand the medium of drama. This imaginary world becomes real, subject to the rules of real life and moving at life's pace, but offering the possibility of greater control. It is our drama—we decide—no one can take it away from us.

Children rarely forget what they have created but unlike a painting, a drama cannot be thrown away or lost, it is a part of them and a part of you. Moreover, drama can provide a kind of motivation and stimulation for further learning that is often difficult to achieve in normal classroom activities. It provides a need for accurate information and leads children to the library or to source material searching for facts:

'What do hippos eat?'

'What sort of houses do Zulus live in?'

'How do you sail a ship?' etc.

It inspires poetry, stories and other creative writing and provides contexts for the many and varied uses of the written word—advertisements, posters, bills, petitions, notices, etc.

It leads to a wide variety of pure art work as well as creating opportunities for applied art and crafts. It feeds off and then provides insights into history, geography, religious education, mathematics and science and incorporates related activities such as music, movement and dance.

After children have had an exciting and absorbing experience, they also may want to share it with others and so a natural development is for the class to create a play which tells their unique story and expresses their feelings for an audience of other children or their parents.

How the drama eventually develops depends on the children and their needs and you and yours. Wherever it goes, I am sure you will find it an exhilarating and invigorating experience.